Best Friend for Life

Best Friend for Life

75 SIMPLE WAYS
TO MAKE ME A HAPPY, HEALTHY,
AND WELL-BEHAVED DOG

AS TOLD TO ANNE BOBBY

FOREWORD BY NEIL GAIMAN

Photographs by Jim Dratfield, Petography®

BLACK DOG
& LEVENTHAL
PUBLISHERS
NEW YORK

ISBN-13: 978-1-57912-593-6

Library of Congress Cataloging-in-Publication Data

Bobby, Anne.
Best friend for life: 75 simple ways to make me a happy,
healthy, and well-behaved dog/as told to Anne Bobby.
p. cm.
ISBN-13 978-1-57912-593-6 (paperback)
1. Dogs—Training 2. Dogs—Behavior. I. Title.
SF431 .B57 2001
636.7'0887—dc21
2001003644

Book design: Liz Driesbach
Manufactured in China

Published by
Black Dog & Leventhal Publishers, Inc.
151 West 19th Street
New York, New York 10011

Distributed by
Workman Publishing Company
225 Varick Street
New York, New York 10014

b d f g e c a

This book is dedicated to Francis DiPietro,

The lost souls still searching for a home,

And those tireless individuals who will always

have room in their hearts for one more.

And, with love and fondest memories, to Prospect.

My Best Girl.

I miss you. I always will.

Foreword

BY NEIL GAIMAN

There are dog people and there are cat people. I was a cat person. I liked their self-confidence, the way they wanted food and would demand affection when they needed it but were, essentially, living their own lives at the edge of my world.

Dogs were needy. Dogs needed love and walking and obedience school. Dogs barked and jumped up on you and you'd never be able to go anywhere again. They smelled like dogs. The big ones looked like wolves and the small ones looked like rats and they shed all over the place.

The only dog in my family was an aunt's, and it was mangy and wandered the town looking for something to mate with. I was hired once as a dog walker for an afternoon, when I was about twelve. I got lost and was gone for hours. My aunt paid up, but that really was the beginning and the end of my canine interaction for many years.

🐾 CABAL, unlike his dad, eschews black leather jackets—especially in hunting season.

Photo: N. Gaiman

Anne Bobby is different.

I've known Anne for about half her lifetime. And I've walked places with her. It may or may not be true that Anne has never met a dog she did not like. It is certainly true that she has never failed to meet a dog. Any dog. If you follow Anne through Brooklyn, or through New York, your progress will be a series of starts and stops as she meets dogs. She stops, she talks to them. I assume that they talk to her. She may ask the person on the other end of the leash what the dog's name is, in order to greet it properly, but she has no other interest in them. She wants to meet the dog. The dog wants to meet her. It's love, over and over and over again. (Her sister Kate was walking with Anne once, and after an Anne–dog encounter, commented on how very attractive the young man holding the leash had been, and how very taken he had been with Anne. And Anne had to confess that she hadn't noticed the human at all.) Anne is someone who volunteers at an animal hospital for fun, and comes home from the hospital at 4:00 A.M., after a long day of hard work, shaken and crying because an animal could not be saved, and then goes back the next night and does it again.

The trouble is that, walking with Anne, her empathy becomes contagious.

I was driving home about five months ago when I noticed a very large, dirty, wet, white, wolflike animal at the side of the road in the rain, about to wander up onto the freeway. So I stopped and got it into the Mini, ignoring the mud and trying to ignore the mixed smells of farmyard and wet dog, and drove it to the Humane Society. And when I learned that his owner, an elderly farmer, kept him on a short chain in a farmyard, thought he was a nuisance, and said that whoever found him could keep him, I didn't really stop to think.

It's been five months, and it's me and a three-year-old white German Shepherd. I've taken him to obedience school, coped with his terror of thunderstorms and elevators, seen the most amazing things while on walks through the woods with him, and found myself part of a very small pack, which consists of me (biped, opposable thumbs, can't smell much) and Cabal (quadruped, huge grin, smells everything). I have a house that is now divided into the dog half (downstairs) and the cat half (upstairs).

Worse. When I go on the road, I miss him.

And when I have a dog-training question, the first thing I do is call Anne, and she tells me everything I need to know, her answers ranging from Wrap It in Cream Cheese to Try Sprinkling Vinegar on It First, and she has been right about everything so far, except for the vinegar. She is convinced that I really, really want to sleep in the same bed as my dog, and seems unwilling to believe that I'm actually extremely happy that the dog is quite willing to sleep on the floor beside the bed, as long as he knows that I'm somewhere around.

You're going to learn about dogs and their people from Anne. She knows her stuff. After all, she's spoken to every dog in Brooklyn.

Confessions of a Dog Listener

BY ANNE BOBBY

My friends don't like hanging around with me very much.

We can be on a street, in a park, on a subway. We can be deep in discussion about anything from what constitutes the perfect pizza to how to cure hiccups, to the influence of the Emperor Trajan's city planning on today's shopping mall.

Then I'll see a dog and my thoughts devolve to the mental consistency of yesterday's oatmeal. My mind struggles, and fails, to hold any thought beyond finding out if that dog has something to say to me.

I look into that dog's eyes and I am lost to anything but the universe that is her experience.

It's usually around that point that whoever I'm with rolls his eyes, mutters something barbed and justified, and, occasionally, walks away. I barely notice. I am deep in a completely different conversation. With a completely different species.

I don't know what a "Dog Whisperer" is, although I've been called that often enough. "Dog Whisperer" sounds masterful, wise—like Someone Who Can Tell Dogs What Is Best. I'm bad at returning phone calls. I can't get my cat to stop chewing holes in my towels. I think meat, for the most part, tastes terrible. I don't like swimming. I never floss.

There's not a whole lot I can teach a dog.

I suppose what I am is a "Dog *Listener*." I've listened to them for years in my Brooklyn neighborhood. I've rescued dogs, played with other people's dogs, weaned dogs, held dogs in my arms as they've breathed their last, and spent nights beyond number with abandoned strays in temporary shelters. They've filled my heart. They've broken my heart. They've stopped my heart.

They've told me when they're happy, when they're scared, when they want to play. When they're bored.

They've told me what they like and what they don't.

I've listened to a stray dog in a cage tell me he's afraid to come close. After a while, he'll tell me where he likes to be petted the most, and what toy is his favorite. And how much he appreciates my love for him.

I've listened to dogs tied up outside stores who think their moms or dads are never coming back for them.

I've listened to dogs who love more deeply than most people I know. Dogs who laugh and cry and yearn and struggle and triumph.

I've listened to old dogs and puppies, sick dogs and wise dogs. Aloof philosophers, walking wounded, and wingnuts with senses of humor that would make a stand-up comic retire his mike.

This book is the result of my countless conversations with these awesome animals, as well as my many years in parks and alleys, in hospitals and on highways, forever dropping to the ground and talking to four-footed strangers.

I am thrilled to share with you the things that dogs want us all to know, and am honored to serve as their translator.

Enjoy their words. I do.

Photo: T. Berry

Tribute to a Dog

This speech was made in 1870 by Senator Gordon Vest of Missouri, at the trial of a man accused of shooting another man's dog. It was his closing argument.

The best friend a man has in the world may turn against him and become his enemy. His son or daughter that he has reared with loving care may prove ungrateful. Those who are nearest and dearest to us, those whom we trust with our happiness and our good name, may become traitors to their faith. The money that a man has, he may lose. It flies away from him, perhaps when he needs it most. A man's reputation may be sacrificed in a moment of ill-considered action. The people who are prone to fall on their knees to do us honor when success is with us, may be the first to throw the stone of malice when failure settles its cloud upon our heads.

The one absolutely unselfish friend that man can have in this selfish world, the one that never deserts him, the one that never proves ungrateful or treacherous, is his dog. A man's dog stands by him in prosperity and in poverty, in health and in sickness. He will sleep on the cold ground, where the wintry winds blow and the snow drives fiercely, if only he may be near his master's side. He will kiss the hand that has no food to offer; he will lick the wounds and sores that come in encounter with the roughness of the world. He guards the sleep of his pauper master as if he were a prince. When all other friends desert, he remains. When riches take wings, and reputation falls to pieces, he is as constant in his love as the sun in its journey through the heavens.

If fortune drives the master forth an outcast in the world, friendless and homeless, the faithful dog asks no higher privilege than that of accompanying him, to guard him against danger, to fight against his enemies. And when the last scene of all comes, when death takes his master in its embrace and his body is laid away in the cold ground, no matter if all his other friends pursue their way, there by the graveside will the noble dog be found, his head between his paws, his eyes sad but open in alert watchfulness, faithful and true even in death.

The plaintiff won his case.

🐾 The South American Maned Wolf looks more like a fox, and is an endangered relative of both dogs and wolves. There are only 1,500 or so of them left in the wild but, thanks to the extraordinary work and dedication of the Durrell Wildlife Conservation Trust, to date GUS and EVA have sired three litters of pups, which ensures the survival of their species! To learn more about Durrell, go to www.durrellwildlife.org

Photos: G. Guida

1. With boundaries and routine, every joy is possible.

Any age, any breed, any size, there are two things we count on you to provide, as important as the food, shelter, and love you've already given.

BOUNDARIES: Let us know we are safe to explore, test ourselves, and learn, for you are there to protect us from harm. Reassure us that you'll never let us eat what we shouldn't or try something that could harm us or feel that we're ever in danger.

ROUTINE: When we know which things in life will always be there, we grow confident, happy, and open to new things, people, and experiences.

SAM is a Cairn Terrier who loves to hike, to carry big sticks, and even small dogs!

Photo: courtesy R. Cholakian

2. We all need training, and we want it, too!

In every little dog beats the heart of a wolf (and every big dog thinks he fits in a teacup—or at least in your lap). That is why, no matter what size we are, you've got to train us. Training doesn't just ensure that a Great Dane won't pull her owner's arm out of the socket. It also allows a Pomeranian to coexist happily with people and socialize well with his buddies. So make sure we're trained—it may save our lives!

🐾 Life on the streets may have been hard for RUFFIAN, but this Chihuahua has gone on to become an agility title holder—thanks to training and love.

Photo: Tien Tran, courtesy D. Seltzer

3. We've been eating raw meat for thousands of years.

Well, what do you think dogs do in the wild . . . open cans? Did you know that "dog food" as we know it didn't even exist until after World War II?

Raw meat—good healthily raised chicken and beef (and don't forget the vegetables!)—has been a part of the dog's diet for centuries. This food is delicious to us, and there are plenty of guidebooks and Web sites that offer advice on how best to prepare our meals. Be sure to consult my veterinarian about my nutrition plan, and keep up with my physical exams (to make sure I don't have any special needs). And DON'T forget to get me used to any new diet GRADUALLY (see Tip 17).

Then watch how a REAL dog eats!!!

🐾 Tibetan Terrier POOBAH eats lots of raw food, and it shows—he's a show champion!

Photo: M. Garrett

4. Some of us can be therapy dogs.

Does your dog love attention?

Is he laid back and not jumpy or nervous, especially around strangers?

Are people always stopping you on the street to play with your dog?

Do you and he have some free time to spend helping people in hospitals or nursing homes?

Guide dogs, service dogs, and K-9 dogs are great—but we regular, everyday dogs can be "volunteers," too. There are many organizations that train animals (and their owners) to visit the sick, the lonely, and people who miss their own pets.

DogPlay.com is a great place to start. They've got lots of ideas about how a smart and sociable dog like me can have fun AND make a difference.

See you in class!

🐾 By the time you read this, Yellow Lab YANKEE will be an official service dog for a disabled person! He owes his great training—and loving nature—to everyone at Puppies Behind Bars (puppiesbehindbars.com).

Photo: H. Bolston

5. When walking me, talk to me.

Sometimes you guys mistake quantity time for quality time, when it comes to walking us. Remember, that for us, walk time is one of the best times of the day, our chance to relax and hang out with you.

When you bring along your cell phone or your iPod, well, it makes our special time a little . . . less special. Maybe you could leave the music at home now and then, and see how much better we are at conversation than anyone you'll find on that phone.

TELL your dog how much YOU enjoy your time together. TALK to him when you walk him. Bring a toy along, have some fun. It will give both of you something to look forward to next time. It sure works for me!

When taking her walk, Lab-mix PAX likes to jump in puddles with her mom and dad!

Photo: L. & A. Morris

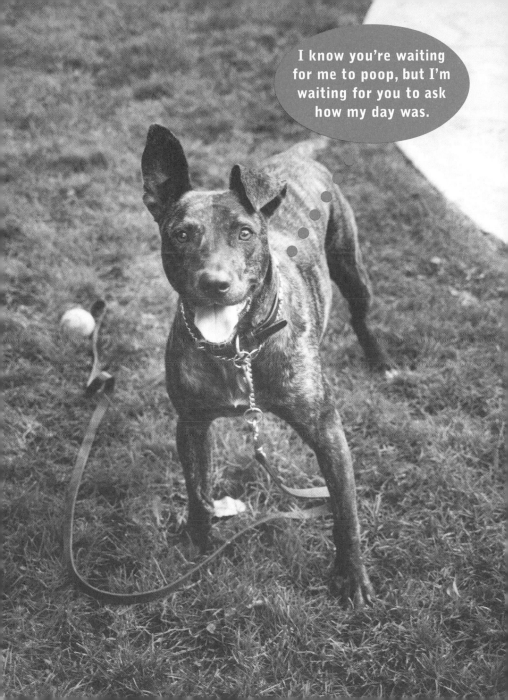

6. If you *have* to duck into the store and leave me outside, leave me in charge of something.

For you, it's a quick stop at the deli—for us, it sometimes feels like the end of the world. I don't know a single one of us who likes being left outside a store. It leaves us vulnerable to strangers, and may make us act in ways we don't like. But if you have to go inside somewhere and leave your dog tied up nearby, leave him in charge of something of yours—a scarf, a glove, a newspaper, or a small package you've picked up along the way. Whatever it is, it will bear your scent and might help calm him down.

Watching over something of yours also makes us feel like a useful part of your team. (And MAKE SURE your dog is wearing tags and has an ID chip implant or tattoo ID!)

🐾 She's a long way from the Humane Society in Vieques, Puerto Rico, but Chihuahua-mix RAMONA has taken to her Brooklyn life with gusto, enjoying both shopping and socializing down at the pub with her friends.

Photo: S. White, M. Lapthorn

7. The more you *talk* to me, the more I'll listen.

Sometimes all it takes is the proper tone of voice. We're very sensitive, you know, and anxiety or tension in a voice can make the more, shall we say, *attuned* dog freak out a bit.

Try using a special tone of voice just for speaking to me, and call me by name as much as possible. Who doesn't want to hear his name on the lips of the person he loves? I sure do! Give that a try the next time I don't seem to want to pay attention. Keep your voice light and pleased, and use a gentle, almost musical sound when you call my name. That will be a reward all its own!

 Former pound puppy **AMBROSE** is a Lab mix who lives for his dog bed and his mom's lap!

Photo: E. Barrows

8. If I eat my poop, I may need a change in my diet.

First things first—many of us eat poops. And yes, it's pretty gross. But it may also mean that we are lacking digestive enzymes and need our diet to be supplemented with enzyme-containing foods such as pumpkin (take the seeds out if your dog is small!) or pineapple. Mixing meat tenderizers into our food is another way of getting us to stop eating our poop.

I've got to be honest, though. None of these things seems to stop us from eating somebody else's. It's just one of those things. I mean, come on, you'll never explain what's so great about coffee; we can't explain the thing with poop!

🐾 After surviving being thrown from a car, Chihuahua TWELVE figures she can eat pretty much whatever she wants!

Photo: J. Martineau

9. Harnesses are great for "tuggers."

You know now how important it is for us to take a class or two (see Tip 2). That's the first step toward keeping us from tugging on our leashes (and your arm socket). But for lots of us, training isn't always enough. Even little dogs have MIGHTY strong shoulders. No wimpy little leash can stop us from tugging the way a harness can—because harnesses catch us *behind our shoulders,* which puts us a little off balance when you tug back! I know they're a little tricky to get on us sometimes but, with practice, it gets easier, especially once we figure out that when you break out the harness, it's time for a walk!

That said—traditional harnesses are no match for medium and larger dogs, especially if their owners aren't heavyweights. "Front-connection" harnesses, such as the Easy Walk from Gentle Leader and the Sense-ation and Sense-ible harnesses, put dogs with strong

🐾 Dachshund/Spaniel/Terrier–mix JAX loves his harness—and his wheels! His favorite activities are hiking, running after his ball, and chasing the horses in Central Park!

Photo: C. Rosenthal

🐾 Chocolate Lab SADIE howls in her sleep! She's probably dreaming of the beach, since her favorite pastime is riding waves.

Photo: J. Cheris

upper bodies off balance by catching them *in front of their shoulders* and low enough on their chest to avoid hurting the esophagus, the way a collar can.

Of course, some dogs will always respond best to prong collars, and when used correctly they are just as invaluable (see Tip 53).

The most important thing to know is that WE WANT you to enjoy walking with us as much as we enjoy walking with you. Let's find the best and safest way to make that happen!

10. Exercise is fun— and good for us both.

Take a good look. Am I fat?

Look, we don't need to go to a gym, for crying out loud, but if you can't see my ribs a little bit, and I have no waist, and "I don't do stairs," then I am probably overweight.

It's not a punishment if you put me on an exercise regimen, especially if you're part of it.

Let's go jogging together!

Let's toss a few balls!

Remember how much you loved Frisbees as a kid? Show me!

(Just make sure we don't overdo it on the first day—and that you keep the vet aware of our new exercise plan.)

After all, we both want to be around for a long, LONG time.

🐾 **CLIFF** is a Labrador who loves running in the yard—but not as much as he loves watching it from his spot on the couch.

Photo: K. Furman

11. Summer Haircuts: The Facts

EVERYBODY seems to have an opinion, don't they?

YES, YES, YES! Shaving a longer-haired dog in the summer is GREAT! It makes me feel better and, so long as you USE THAT SUN-SCREEN, I'll have a more comfortable time.

NO, NO, NO! A dog's coat insulates him not only from the cold, but ALSO from the HEAT! Our bodies aren't the same as yours, you know. I'd rather count on YOU to know when I'm hot and ready for a jump in the lake or a shower from the hose. I might even push myself too hard if I don't have my fur coat on as a warning to myself to SLOW DOWN.

For ME, it's best to keep that fur coat on. But again, every dog—just like every person—is different.

Now turn on that fan, and get me a bully stick. (A what? You'll see: read Tip 20!)

 Don't take scissors to the fur of MISTER BO JANGLES! This Champion Papillon LOVES the way he looks—he grooms himself in the mirror!

Photo: C. Jones

12. Neutering can add years to my life—and ease my stress!

You probably know that intact males are more likely to fight because of the effect of testosterone on their behavior. But an intact dog can actually become a victim of neutered dogs, who sometimes feel threatened by the scent of testosterone. Intact dogs also run a higher risk of getting prostate infections and testicular cancer. And, let's just say that the number of unneutered dogs that run away in search of some "satisfaction" is cause enough for *me* to speak out in favor of neutering your male dog!

🐾 **TESSA** is a Spinone Italiano who loves to chew the ears of her boyfriend, Golden Retriever **QUINCY**—who happens to be neutered.

Photo: courtesy D. Solomon

13. If you want to keep me off the furniture, be sure I have a special place of my own to hang out in.

Crates aren't just for travel, you know—after all, who doesn't need a little privacy now and then? If you don't want me to treat your furniture like my personal boudoir, set up my crate and show me that I have a room of my own. I'll feel important, and it's a great way of helping me adjust to the fact that there are some places in the house that are just yours.

The crate is also a helpful solution for those of us who get all stressed out at bedtime. Just keep it near your bed, throw in a few toys and a blanket—and leave the door open!

 Border Collie–mix OSO is a contemplative "philosopher-dog" with a favorite place to lay his head—the sunniest patch of the porch.

Photo: D. Gillman

14. A treat secret from the pros.

What tiny treat do the best dog handlers use to get us to pose at dog shows? What nutritious tidbit is high in protein and extremely tasty to us? What inexpensive morsel can be crushed up and sprinkled over our food when we're feeling finicky? What treat will we do ANYTHING for?

Freeze-dried Beef Liver, available at any pet store. (By the way, cats love it, too!) For variety, try freeze-dried chicken—some of us like that even more!

🐾 Squirrelly the squeak toy may not be edible, but LUCY the Pug takes her everywhere.

Photo: S. Fox

15. You're wearing sunscreen. I need it, too.

Middle of summer? We're going out for a picnic? Great! How about you spread a little of that sunblock around? Sure, we get sunburned, too—especially light-colored and short-haired dogs. Protect me from harmful rays by applying a little sunblock around my nose and ears. Be sure to rub it in, though, because I might try to make a snack of it. You might even want to use it when I'm indoors if I'm one of those dogs who *lives* in the sunniest spots in the house!

🐾 Chocolate Lab **FANNIE** knows that summer is the best time to swim across her favorite lake—a mile wide!

Photo: J. Beaver

16. If you don't catch me "in the act," it won't do any good to discipline me later.

You come home after work.

I've eaten your paycheck for lunch.

You yell.

I don't know why. I know it's tough, but the only time you should reprimand me for any behavior you don't like is THE MOMENT I've done it. After that, I have no idea what it is you're unhappy about. I won't understand why you're saying "naughty girl"—I may think it's because I just gave you a kiss. Now, you don't want me to stop *that*, do you?

If I'm doing something you really need to break me of, try "baiting" me: set up a situation where you are likely to catch me in the act—then let me know. (And check out Tip 62. It's all about praising me when I get it right!)

🐾 If only MAGGIE didn't look so cute after making a snack of her dad's glasses.

Photo: J. P. Leventhal

17. We are sensitive to changes in our kibble—so don't disrupt our diet routine too much.

When it comes to store-bought dry and wet foods, changing my diet can result in diarrhea unless you get me used to my new food gradually, by mixing it in with my old food. Try not to mess with a good thing more often than you have to. I'll thank you for that boring breakfast every morning!

(That's not to say I don't like my food supplemented by some new things, as you've already read in Tip 3. And check out Tip 35 for even more great ideas!)

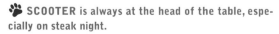
🐾 **SCOOTER** is always at the head of the table, especially on steak night.

Photo: A. Wallach

18. Dog play can look rough— watch my body language.

Fact one: Dogs *love* to play with each other. Fact two: Dogs at play resemble dogs at war. That doesn't mean you should interfere, or that we need to be separated. Watch our body language when we play— are our tails wagging? Are we trading off submissive and playful postures (rolling on our sides, arching our front paws and chests to the ground)? Are we nipping at each other's ears and tails, and NOT at eyes and back legs? We'll let you know when we've had enough. Watch us for bristled fur, fangs, and staring with lunging—those are bad signs. Listen for growling and persistent, urgent barking. Honestly, if all you see and hear is a lot of jumping and hitting the deck, we're probably just having a good time. Cross my heart!

🐾 **GINGER** (l.) and **APPLE** (r.), a Pit mix and Staffordshire Terrier, may look scary when they play, but in fact they are inseparable best friends.

Photo: H. Knight, R. & J. Freibrunn

No worries here!

19. We get anxious, too!

Just like you, I sometimes feel nervous or anxious. Have you ever heard of Rescue Remedy? It's a great homeopathic solution made of plant essences, designed to help with anxiety. It was created a long time ago for people, but veterinarians have been using it on cats and dogs for years! Just put a drop on my nose for me to lick off, or on my food. It will help me deal with all of life's little worries!

Rescue Remedy also comes in cream form, which is great to apply on scratches, bruises, and rashes, along with any medications my vet prescribes.

 When Shepherd-mix MINGUS isn't dancing or swimming, you can usually find him shelling his own pistachios.

Photo: K. Michel, B. Vye

20. As a special treat, give me a bully stick.

Brace yourself. You may not like this, but I sure do. Once a week or so—as often as *you* might have a sundae or a cigar—try giving your best friend a bully stick. You don't want to know what it is (okay, it's a dried bull penis), but we LOVE them. They're softer than rawhides and break down in our stomachs better, so they won't harm us (unless you give us too many; then we get the runs). They're also full of protein and they taste good and . . . you know what? They're our favorite!

🐾 Norwich Terrier **BUDDY** will do anything his dad says, before he says it, when there's a bully stick at stake!

Photo: L. Willard

21. Know when it's time to call my doctor.

No one ever said you should take us to the vet every time we sneeze. But if we're showing certain symptoms, please don't try to practice first aid on us! Call or take your dog to the vet if:

- Your dog has been limping for more than 24 hours.
- Your dog has been bitten. (Many people wait too long on this one!)
- Your dog has had diarrhea for more than 72 hours, with no other symptoms.
- Your dog has bloody diarrhea and is vomiting.
- Your dog has diarrhea accompanied by loss of appetite and vomiting.
- Your dog is bleeding.
- Your dog is having difficulty breathing.
- There is any sign of diarrhea or vomiting accompanied by fever.
- You've noticed any change in your dog's appearance or demeanor.

 Former junkyard dog **RACE** was hit by a car and left to die. Then he was rescued. The accident may have cost the Shepherd mix his back right leg, but he got a loving home in exchange.

Photo: M. McInerny

22. Making eye contact can be REALLY fun!

To me, eye contact is like a challenge, and I try to avoid looking another dog in the eyes for too long. There's a *great* game that shows you how to use that to my advantage! It's fun for puppies and shy dogs, and it's an easy way to coax older and, shall we say, *less svelte* dogs into getting off their behinds. Start walking around and calling, "Where's Sheba? Sheba, where'd you go?" When Sheba comes running, don't make eye contact. Just keep calling, "Sheba! Sheba!" and Sheba will start to follow you and jump and spin for you, trying to catch your eye.

It sounds so simple, doesn't it? Well, sometimes that's exactly what the best things are—REALLY simple!

 ELSA has a game of her own. Every time her mom opens the blinds, this Shepherd mix spins around and around, howling with joy!

Photo: A. Kato-Culp

23. Did you know?
I'm lactose intolerant!

Some of us lack the enzyme that breaks down dairy products. I won't go into excruciating detail here, but sometimes feeding guys like me milk or milk products can lead to some embarrassing moments. You'll know *your* dog is lactose intolerant by watching out for diarrhea. Don't let me have that milk shake—no matter how much I say I've earned it!

(If she's not lactose intolerant, a little bit of dairy isn't so bad for her—and there's something REALLY special in yogurt. Take a look at Tip 42!)

🐾 NICKY is a Poodle with brains AND beauty—
he's an agility champion!

Photo: J. Fields

24. Help me learn that a new baby is *my* family, too.

Bringing home a new baby? Here's a great way to help introduce me to her. (Get ready. It's a two-person operation.) Have Mom come in first. Give us a chance to say hi—it's been a while, after all, and she has this interesting, different, new-person smell all over her. Let us go into the yard together for some extended greeting and play, or maybe we can take a nice walk. While we're out, here's your job, Dad. Start scattering the baby's things around the house. The blankets, the car seat, the burpy-cloth. They all carry the baby's scent, and make me feel as if she's already part of the family and home I love and protect. You might also want to wrap the baby in something that smells like you, a blanket you've slept in or a T-shirt you've worn. That way, when we finally do meet, this new little person will already smell like an old friend.

 Shepherd-mix MAGRITTE took no time to fall in love with her best buddy, Garreth, and even less time to bond with his sister, Collette!

Photo: K. O'Brien

28. The First-Aid Kit

I'm not saying we need a whole medicine cabinet, but these are the ten things that every dog-owner should definitely have on hand at all times, so that your vet or the National Animal Poison Center can better assist you in an emergency:

1. Mineral oil (as a laxative)
2. Tweezers
3. Gauze pads, tape, and a roll of gauze bandaging
4. Cotton balls (NOT synthetic cosmetic puffs but PURE COTTON, for certain obstructions)
5. Hydrogen peroxide (to induce vomiting)
6. Betadine
7. A tube of antibacterial cream
8. A rectal thermometer
9. Any medications prescribed by your veterinarian, and the tele-

🐾 Maltese-mix **FORTUNATO** is aptly named.
He recovered from a terrible car accident with the help of his friends...

Photos: W. Loomis

phone numbers of your vet and the Animal Poison Control Center (in case your dog is in someone else's care at the time of the emergency)

10. A book of first aid for dogs

Take a moment and make sure that you have these things in your house, and that they are in a convenient place—and always make sure that any dog-walker or dog-sitter knows where these things are. They could help save my life someday!

🐾 ...Maltipoo LILY and Shepherd-mix HANNA.

Photos: W. Loomis

26. I was here first. It's important that I know I haven't been replaced in your heart.

When you bring home a new dog or cat, let *me* come around to accepting him first. Give him hugs in private, when I'm not around to see. Your support and attention to ME during my period of adjustment will let me know that having a new face in the family doesn't mean you love me less. Whenever there's a new arrival—whether it's a cute kitten or a little guy who smells like formula—you need to spend a lot of quality time with me. You'd be surprised how insecure some of us can be. (I know, I know, I act more like the Clint Eastwood type!)

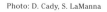 Dachshunds **LUCY** and **ETHEL** have always gotten along. Ethel was born with one ear—honest.

Photo: D. Cady, S. LaManna

27. The Dog Run

For urban dogs, socializing is very often done at "dog runs"—special areas in parks or neighborhoods that have been set aside for dogs and their owners to use for exercise and play. But even country dogs enjoy getting together with their buddies for a little bit of supervised "touch tail"! It's a privilege to have a socializing space nearby, and there are some simple ways to make visiting any dog run a pleasant experience for all!

1. Be responsible for me. I'll go anywhere you take me, you know. It's up to you to decide whether or not I'm capable of playing well in a group. Some dogs are "solo artists"—don't try and change us and don't try to force a situation that will make fellow pups uncomfortable.

2. Keep it clean. Even if you and I are the *only* ones there . . . c'mon, use the plastic bag. That will make us all happy and help keep us from making a snack of something we shouldn't. Have you considered setting up a little "cleaning corner" with extra plastic bags, a trash can, a rake or shovel—maybe even a compost bin—at your local run?

3. Keep me calm. If I've got some special toy that I can't live without, maybe it would be better if we left it at home. I mean, heck, I can make a toy of just about anything. I'd rather you bring something I wouldn't mind the other guys taking off with. We're all pretty democratic *most* of the time—but we're not any different from people: sometimes we get grabby.

4. Ease me in. If your dog is new, bring him to the run at a less crowded time at first, and watch him for signs of stress. Arrange playdates with dogs that make a favorable impression, and be mindful of situations that make him uneasy.

5. Include an outsider. If you see a dog having difficulty getting into the group, try to include both the dog and the owner. If the dog is the same size as me, maybe we can hang out. Don't let some poor owner think he's a failure just because his dog doesn't have the greatest social skills—the dog could end up paying a hefty price.

6. Let me into the fray. Okay, so if I have a choice between sitting with my tennis ball or running with the bulldogs (and shepherds and mastiffs), guess where I'll probably want to be? That's the great thing about a dog run—EVERYBODY's a quarterback, no matter his or her size. That's how dogs play, so don't bring me if you're worried about my ending up in a scrimmage. Organize a small-dog playdate at the run if your pug wants to pick on someone his own size!

7. Watch ME! Yes, you! You think I don't care if you see me get the stick from the Basset Hound who tackled me last week? I CARE—so put down that phone, stop flirting, and WATCH ME BE A HERO!

 MAGNOLIA is a deeply protective seven-pound Chihuahua who will try to attack anything larger than she is, except for other Chihuahuas and unfixed males of any size.

Photo: S. Krieger

28. Make sure the ball I'm catching is safe.

Is that a tennis ball I see? Away with it! Yeah, I know—I used to like them, too. Then I heard about how tennis balls are made of sand, and how they can grind my teeth down. Tricky, huh? I mean, they even sell them in great doggie flavors. But, no—if you're going to throw me a ball, make sure it's one that's safe for me. We really like those high-bouncy blue rubber balls (just make sure you get the right size—your pet store owner will help).

By the way, the Ball Launcher (from Chuckit) will send that ball even farther—and save your shoulder!

🐾 **Bullmastiff/Pit—mix LEO** is a big fan of Koosh Balls—and hanging out with his buddies at his local bagel shop.

Photo: J. Greenwald

29. Finding a great dog-walker

Okay, okay, I KNOW you can't ALWAYS be there for my walks. Or maybe you know how much I love to walk and you want to make sure I'm spoiled rotten with an extra walk a day! How do you pick my new walking buddy?

Well, of course word-of-mouth is great. Ask friends at your dog run or ask my vet. (You may even find that my favorite veterinary technician is a great dog-walker!) Or just keep an eye out for a dog-walker you see every day.

DON'T be afraid to interview him/her EXTENSIVELY. If he is as good as he says he is, he won't mind answering your questions. (Some dog-walkers are even bonded and insured.)

If your dog-walker walks any of my friends, see if we can go out together for a little extra gossip time! If you're gone a lot, you might

🐾 Toy Poodle ROXY goes to work with her mom every day—but she's never met a person she didn't like!

Photo: S. Bott

want to look into a doggie day-care facility or dog spa near your home or workplace. Be sure to interview them just as carefully.

If I'm an older dog, or have special needs (sweaters, raingear, booties), make sure your stand-in knows how to dress me up to go out, too.

And . . . be sure to ask me how I feel. See how I get along with my new friend. After all, I love going outside, but someone has to be pretty special to take your place when I take a walk!

🐾 **Rotti/Lab-mix ARROW loves anyone—anyone who doesn't try to take his Kong, that is!**

Photo:S. Greenhoe

30. What to Do If You Think I'm a Star

Do I draw a crowd on walks? Do I listen especially well to commands, or have a few special tricks? How am I at memorizing? (Kidding!)

If you think I've got what it takes, and YOU want to do it as much as you think I do, here are a few things you should know before you start me off on the road to FAME.

- Most agencies and film studios will require proof of my excellent behavior in the form of the American Kennel Club's (AKC.org) Canine Good Citizen Certification. It's a sort of school for stars-in-the-making—we even get a "diploma"!

- PLEASE make sure you check out ANY agency VERY carefully: there are all sorts of laws out there to protect me, which any good agent will follow.

🐾 Pit Bull MURPHY survived a terrible truck accident when he was only two. He's grown up happy and healthy, snuggling and giving the best kisses ever!

Photo: C. Colucci

- Be wary of any agency that wants you to put up a whole lot of money for one of its classes. But know that having a star in the house can be expensive travel-wise, grooming-wise, and ESPE-CIALLY time-wise. For both of us.

Don't forget—modeling is WORK (even though not every dog sees it that way). If you think I'd be happier with a less strict schedule—and less traveling—I may like being a THERAPY DOG better. (Check out Tip 4!)

🐾 Shepherd-mix PRISCILLA loves to pose, especially when there's a cookie involved. But she's happiest as the greeter at her mom's bookstore!

Photo: A. Bobby

31. Some kinds of fruit can send me to the hospital.

You kidding? I love fruit! Trouble is, some fruit doesn't love me. Did you know that many big dogs end up needing surgery because they've swallowed peach and mango pits? Did you know that apple seeds contain cyanide in an amount that could be fatal to a small dog? Did you know that grapes and raisins are toxic for pups? Fruit can and should be a wonderful dietary supplement (coconut, for example, is a great source of vitamins), but please be careful about keeping that fruit bowl out of my reach. I'll thank you for it!

🐾 HENRY takes his diet seriously—he spits out anything he doesn't like, including some fruit!

Photo: Anne Burns

32. Don't laugh—everyone loves a massage.

It's a wonderful feeling, getting my ears rubbed. And my shoulders—gosh, have you any idea how much weight I'm carrying around? And my toes, they're all tense from grabbing at the ground and digging in, especially when I jump into the air and sneak a bite of whatever you're eating. Spend a little time getting to know which part of *your* dog's body needs some kneading, and give that buddy of yours a rubdown whenever you can.

Massage time is also a great time to get me used to "dummy clippers"—see Tip 45!

🐾 When she isn't off hunting squirrels, Greyhound-mix ZORA is probably looking to get her belly rubbed.

Photo: M. Harrison, H. Scarbrough

33. Give us these projects and watch us go!

Here's a great game for the big-time chewer: Take a favorite smelly treat (a liver treat is great for this, or a little piece of salami). Find a rag and knot the treat inside. Make as many knots as you can, and then give it to me. Watch how many hours I spend working that one out!

Depending on my size and strength, you can make the game even more interesting. First, cut some paw-sized holes in a small cardboard box; then put two or three of the treat puzzles inside, and seal the box. I'll have a great time trying to fish for them! Just be sure to supervise me—especially if I'm little. I could live in a box if there's a treat inside!

 There's no end to the potential treats for Shepherd-mix ELLA. Mom and Dad own a restaurant!

Photo: M. Pisciotta

34. Keep me on the leash for regular walks.

When it comes to leashes and walks, you and I may disagree. I know you don't want me to feel "restricted," that you think a leash curtails my freedom when we walk. But trust me, I don't see my leash as a torture implement. My leash is my way of keeping track of you. When you take my leash away, I have to keep making sure that you haven't run off or gotten in trouble. Don't worry, I'll enjoy feeling "free" when we get to the park. When we're out just walking, let's stay connected. It helps me show the rest of the world that we belong to each other.

🐾 Collie-mix **PADRAIC** was found trying to sneak into his local Saint Patrick's Day parade. Now he watches from the sidewalk—with his family.

Photo: C. Claremont, B. Fleisher

35. Organic is great for you AND me!

"Organic" isn't just for people. Organic pet food tastes great, is easy to get, AND is a great way to avoid the preservatives and toxins found in other dog food. (Did you know that some chemicals in dog foods can lead to serious illnesses such as liver and kidney failure?)

You can find lots of great companies online that sell natural and organic food. You can also tell your pet-store owner that YOU WANT TO SEE organic food on his shelves. That way, other people will stop and think about giving us good old-fashioned "straight from the farm" dinner, too.

And don't stop there: Lots of people also sell natural and holistic vitamins and treats. There are FANTASTIC products for cats, too, and even fair-trade toys and bedding!

🐾 Best buddies GRACIE (left) and Hudson (right) not only LOVE organic food— they love it RAW! They're also chefs. Visit their Web site (www.hudsonriverdogs.com) for great recipes!

Photos: C. Delaine

I know that healthy, organic food and other stuff can be a little pricier than what you're used to, but hey, I'm worth it, aren't I? Especially when I do that great trick where I eat your shoe?

36. Shelters need volunteers (and other things)!

There are SO many ways to help my abandoned friends find the owners of their dreams. Contact your local shelter, or Humane Society or ASPCA and see what they need.

Maybe it's dog walking. Maybe it's cage cleaning. Maybe it's helping at adoption sites or fostering a stray, or driving a dog to a new home far away. It might be driving a dog to the vet . . . and I'm just getting started here; the list goes on and on!

Don't forget that shelters always need things, too, such as towels, toys, bedding, carriers, and extra food. (Just make sure it's all clean and in good condition. After all, we want to make these dogs feel more special than anyone.)

🐾 It took time and patience and the love of lots of people but Akita STELLA is homeless no longer. She loves her new family so much, she stations herself right by the door until everyone is back home each night.

Photo: S. Gladstone

Of course, there's one REEEALLY great way to help a shelter. . . .
See that cute little guy in the last cage on the left? Yeah, he's looking at you, too!

From city life to suburban tranquility,
Pomeranian **FLUFFY (or "FLUFF DADDY")**
was adopted by his forever-family, who know
he's afraid of nothing that comes his way,
not even dogs or motorcycles!

Photo: S. Stiles

37. Whole rawhides can hurt my stomach.

Did you know that rawhides could be hazardous to my health? I might break off sharp pieces and swallow them and, since rawhide doesn't break down in my stomach, it could irritate my digestive tract. If your dog really likes rawhide, make sure any chew toy you give him is made from *compressed* rawhide, and get me the kind made in the United States. The South American stuff is very salty and has lots of chemicals in it. Otherwise, try a bone or a bully stick instead (see Tips 28 and 50). Oh—and don't go for the pigs' ears instead! They're just as dangerous as rawhide.

🐾 Pound-rescue pup **SALLY** loves her chew toys so much, she walks her mom and dad right over to the pet store—no matter where they're supposed to be going!

Photo: A. & J. Reinhart

38. Plan our car trips safely.

Don't let me guilt you out, but ... the car is for me *only* when you know I will *never* be left inside unattended. Even a few minutes in an overheated car can cost me my life. Or I might eat something I shouldn't, suffer from hypothermia, or break a window if I get scared. And, while you may like the idea of having your best buddy sitting next to you, admiring how you obey the rules of the road, I belong in my crate—for my own sake.

(Want to take me REALLY far away? See Tip 57 about dogs and airplanes!)

🐾 SPUD loves to be indoors, even in hotel rooms—so long as his mom is with him and somebody left a french fry lying around!

Photo: D. Seltzer

39. You should probably avoid giving me any chocolate.

Everyone's heard how "dogs are allergic to chocolate," that even a little bit of the stuff is dangerous for us. But *why* is that? It's the caffeine in the chocolate, as well as the theobromine (the main alkaloid of the cacao bean) that causes seizures in dogs. There's no fixed amount of chocolate that causes harm—it all depends on my size and the amount I ingest. The general rule is the darker the chocolate, the higher the caffeine content. One 1-ounce bar of Hershey's dark chocolate contains three times as much as its milk-chocolate counterpart; and unsweetened baking chocolate has *ten times* the caffeine of milk chocolate. But really, giving me *any* kind of chocolate is unhealthy. Face it: Chocolate is fattening, it's bad for my teeth, and, if it's got a lot of caffeine and theobromine, it could prove fatal. Next time I'm trying to get you to part with a piece of your brownie, just say NO (nicely, please).

🐾 Lab-mix GINGER (right) and Chocolate Lab MAX (left) don't need caffeine to wake them up—just a quick dip in the pool. (Max dives in, Ginger just dips her paws.)

Photo: Koch family

40. Your dog is your child, and will do childish things.

Not all dogs are as smart as I am. I know the difference between my toys and yours. (Well . . . there was that time I chewed up the contents of your gym bag, but that was because you were spending too much time away from home.) But some dogs just can't stop thinking that what's *yours* is *theirs*. Don't make it harder for the curious dog: Puppy-proof your home and treat her as you'd treat a baby — because that's what she is! Give her lots of toys of her own to play with, reward her with a treat, praise when she does what you ask, and try not to get too angry when she makes an honest mistake. Of course, a little discipline is sometimes called for — boundaries, remember? And if this is the third time she's stuck her head in that fish tank, we're looking at a *serious* "time-out."

🐾 Despite her fondness for "perfectly good chicken carcasses" when she was a puppy, no one ever sent Newfoundland ABBY packing!

Photo: B. Giella

41. Vinegar is good for me.

I can't say enough about how great apple cider vinegar is for me—inside and out!

A teaspoon a day for a forty-pound dog (less for smaller types) mixed in wet food can help entice me to eat if I'm being picky.

If I have a "hot spot," try misting some vinegar on the affected area with a spray bottle.

Putting a few drops in my ears after I've gotten a bath or gone swimming keeps them from getting all smelly. (Some people say that a rinse of equal parts apple cider vinegar and water after a bath helps prevent fleas!)

Vinegar even helps get rid of those tear stains on my light-haired buddies' faces. Just put a few drops into their drinking water!

English Lurcher PRADA nearly died as a puppy but, thanks to a **GREAT** vet, the love of her parents and dog buddies, and a healthy diet, Prada is all grown up and gorgeous!

Photo: L. Guy

42. A bacteria that's good for you—and me!

Did you know that there are certain bacteria living inside us that help aid in digestion? Did you know that if we're taking an antibiotic or have diarrhea or other stomach problems, those bacteria die?

Yogurt can help.

There's this bacteria called (fancy name, here it comes) *Lactobacillus acidophilus* (acidophilus for short). When we eat foods high in acidophilus, it helps take the place of the bacteria that's been killed inside us until it can grow back again.

Yogurt is a GREAT source of acidophilus, and most of us LOVE it! Try giving your dog a teaspoonful. See?

(I know what you're thinking. What about Tip 23? Some of us are lactose intolerant! Fortunately, you can also get us acidophilus supplements. Just ask your vet.)

 For total comfort, Mini Bull Terrier JESSE eschews pajamas, takes the middle of the bed, and enjoys his first latte of the day while propped up on pillows.

Photo: E. Moses

43. How to Make Me the "Employee of the Month"

So you're allowed to bring me to work with you? GREAT! But there are some things you should consider before putting my name on your office door.

Is the trip to work a stressful one for you? Well, imagine what it will be like for a hairy fella like me in a Sherpa bag, and consider whether your commute is safe (and legal) for me.

Do I have a tendency to, ahem, lose control on occasion? If I'm prone to accidents, you may want to consider leaving me at home— with a wee-wee pad, if necessary.

Are some of your coworkers allergic, or opposed to dogs in the workplace? If so, then make sure I am either easily crated or gated or kept at a distance from anyone who might not appreciate my licks and sniffs.

🐾 Maltipoo CLARENCE (left) and Maltese ZUZU (right) love going to work with Mom...

Photo: K. Quackenbush

If you work in a store, or in a place where I may encounter strangers, make sure I am VERY good at following commands (see Tip 55), and that I won't just assume everyone is a fan of mine. You might even want to put a sign up informing people of the four-legged staff member!

And, most important, make sure I'm having fun. Some of us really are "stay-at-home" types. If I show signs of stress at work (loss of appetite, hair loss, nervousness), think about letting me work out of the house and, maybe, getting a dog walker to come to MY workplace.

🐾 ... She's a dog groomer who keeps them both looking fabulous!

Photo: K. Quackenbush

44. I would like the vet more if he didn't do weird things to me every time I saw him.

Do *you* like going to the doctor, where you're poked and prodded and people stick things in *you*? Yeah, and you know *why* it's happening. We don't. That's why every now and then it's a good idea to take me to the vet to "get weighed." No, I'm not fat. "Getting weighed" is code for going to the hospital when everything is fine, so I don't equate the vet with only horrible things and being sick. Call the vet and see if it's okay to swing by sometime just to say hi. You'll be amazed at how much easier it will make our next important visit.

🐾 **Samoyed RIPLEY** loves her vet—after all, that's where she goes to get fluffed!

Photo: C. Schelling

45. Use dummy clippers when you play with me sometimes, and I won't get scared when you really trim my nails.

Is claw clipping a problem in your house? It was in mine—until my dad did something really neat. He bought a set of round clippers and removed the sharp blade. Then, while we were cuddling and he was massaging my toes and brushing me, he got out the "dummy" clippers and "cut" my claws. Now I've gotten so used to having someone messing around with my toes, I get less scared when he goes at my claws with the real thing. I sometimes can't even tell which is which!

🐾 **ELLA** is a Yellow Lab who loves being groomed, especially with her shedding brush. It helps her look her best when she's riding her skateboard—which she does beautifully!

Photo: E. Sanchez

46. A clicker is a great way to tell me I've done something good.

Have you ever heard of "clickers," little hand-held snapping devices that make this "click" sound? You can find them in pet catalogs and some pet stores, and they're great for telling me when I've made you happy. The second, I mean the very SECOND, I do something you like, just click the clicker and give me a treat. That click helps me "imprint" the moment in my mind. With repetition, I'll figure out that you like it when I don't lunge at an unfamiliar dog, or when I let the baby play with my ears.

Mixed-breed GRIPPER went from "unreachable" by humans to an agility title holder—thanks to love and "clicker" training.

Photo: Tien Tran

47. Remember this number for the National Animal Poison Control Center: 1-888-426-4435.

Have my legs suddenly stopped working, even though I haven't been in any accident you've seen? Do you have macadamia nuts in the house? Or raisins? Did you know that these foods are toxic to me and must be kept out of my reach? There are lots of things in the house that you may not realize are harmful, even fatal, to us dogs—which is why it's a good idea to keep the number of the National Animal Poison Control Center by your phone. By the way, they also have a Web site: www.aspca.org/apcc.

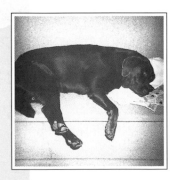

🐾 **ALEXANDRA** is known as the "Crater Creator" at her house—put her ball on the ground outside, and ... well, you can guess what happens next.

Photo: J. Beaver

Now what's the number for pizza?

48. Eventually, we ALL need a pill.

There are LOTS of tricks to giving me a pill (and making sure you don't find it under the bed the next day).

* If your dog is a puppy, it's best to get her used to taking pills right away: open her mouth at her lower jaw, pressing her lips against her teeth and, with her mouth open, give her a REALLY great reward, such as salami or a liver treat. When the time comes that you *need* her to take a pill the same way, she'll be comfortable opening her mouth for you.

* Try keeping any pills your dog takes in the same container as his favorite treat, so the pill absorbs some of the smell.

* Pill Pockets are great—they're these bite-size yummy treats with a little hole in the middle for you to hide my pill in. See if your vet or pet store carries them!

🐾 Black-and-tan DAISY and Cihuahua/Basenji-mix KIRA JOY were found at separate shelters, but they share everything—except pills!

Photo: C. Strumph

- Remember that some of us aren't very good with dairy (see Tip 23). You should avoid hiding my pill in cheese. (Dairy products can reduce the effectiveness of antibiotics, anyway.)

- Ask your vet if my medicine can be crushed and mixed with liquid. If it can, then mix the medicine into a small amount of beef broth or gravy, fill a syringe (your vet can give you one), open my jaw, and wedge it between my back teeth. Then push the plunger. Presto!

- THIS IS IMPORTANT: If YOU'RE nervous about "pilling" me, then I'LL be nervous! Don't be afraid to be firm—it will actually make me feel safer.

Remember: I NEED my medicine, and you NEED to give it to me. Ask our veterinarian for more help if you need it.

49. A little petroleum jelly on my paws will protect me from the snow.

Not all of us dream of pulling a sled. Some of us don't even like cold sidewalks. But did you know that snow—and snow-melting compounds—can irritate my paws? I might not be able to tell you, but they do. In extreme cases you might see me hop around while I'm outside, usually from the salt in the snow, which stings. Before taking me out in the snow, rub a little petroleum jelly into my paws. Better yet (if I'm game), try those winter booties you used to laugh at when you saw them on your neighbor's puppy! While we're on the subject, did you know that I might lick those harmful chemicals and salts off my paws and ingest them? Make sure you keep a pan of clean water by the front door during the winter months, to wash my paws in when I come back inside. That'll keep me on my toes!

 Rescued Border Collie MOWE (rhymes with Joey) loves her off-leash time in the park—any time of year. She's small for her breed (only twenty-five pounds), but that doesn't stop her from herding the Rottweilers and Shepherds she plays with.

Photo: D. Fried, S. Oppenheim

50. Adopting a Shelter Dog

So you want to adopt a stray dog—AWESOME!!!

The exploding population of stray animals has filled shelters with more lost dogs than you can imagine. Taking in a stray dog is both a kindness and a reward, for these dogs are as good at both giving and receiving love as is any dog that is used to a stable home and loving owner. A shelter or pound, however, can be a traumatic place to visit. The sight of dozens, even hundreds, of abandoned animals is heartbreaking.

DON'T LET THAT STOP YOU. Just prepare for the experience and remember that your reward is on the other side of that shelter door.

Don't go to a shelter alone. Bring a friend or ask one of the staff to walk you through. It's good to have someone to help you find the right dog.

DON'T FORGET, you can't save all of them. You can't take every dog home, and you shouldn't. EVERY dog—even the saddest, most

🐾 Terrier-Rottweiler-mix JAGGER was a selective kisser who loved two things—snow and chasing skunks. He was sprayed seven times over his long, happy life, and passed away at a contented thirteen!

Photo: M. Murphy

Short-haired Pointer GRETYL and Black Lab/Pointer–mix COFFEY always want to help others. They learned that from their dad, who's a volunteer fireman.

Photo: J. Gasser

desperate of us—has the right to choose his or her owner. It's got to be the right match, for both our sakes! Many of the dogs you'll meet in the shelter are there because someone took them in recklessly or for emotional reasons, without considering their real needs, and the dog's. This time around, make sure it's for keeps.

51. Some toys NEVER go out of style!

1. **Booda Bones:** The best! Every size, every shape.
2. **Kongs:** We'll play with these for hours. Try smearing some peanut butter in the hole for extra fun.
3. **Velvets:** Great for our gums, too.
4. **Gum Rubber Toys (Rough and Rugged):** They say they're made of "indestructible gum rubber," and they really are tough. Of course, there are dogs that can bite through anything!
5. **Training Ball (VIP):** Best for little dogs and puppies, especially, because they keep moving and so do the dogs. These are great if you want to tire us out!
6. **The Golden Planet Collection:** These "animals from around the world" dolls come from the American Kennel Club, and are made of recy-

🐾 **Of course, there are all sorts of great toys—including Doberman WOODY's pet horse!**

Photo: G. Rivenson

cled polyester. Rabbits, deer, owls, porcupines, mice—you name it—these guys come in ALL sizes!

7. Hard Core Fire Hose (Kyjen Company): These floatable toys are made from actual FIRE HOSES—and you know how tough THEY are! They're filled with rubber and a squeaker, and are really great for teething pups!

8. Zoom Flyers (Planet Dog): There's NOTHING like a Frisbee—and when you get one of these, you're also helping support a REALLY worthy cause. Check them out at www.planetdogfoundation.org.

9. Balls: Who doesn't like a ball? The higher they bounce (and the farther you throw them), the better.

10. You: Well, come on—you know you're the best toy there is!!

 Yellow Lab EMMA has her own idea of toys. She loves sticks so much, she'll drag entire trees into her mom's yard!

Photo: P. Soper

52. Steer clear of antifreeze!

It's one of the more lethal substances to me. Even a trace amount of antifreeze can send me into kidney failure. While the sweet-tasting ethylene glycol in antifreeze may be tempting to me, it breaks down into a compound that is highly toxic to my nervous system. Purchasing pet-safe antifreeze for your car is a good start, but most dangerous of all to me are the green puddles that collect on the street where cars park. Keep me away! (And watch for signs of poisoning: vomiting, lethargy, signs of "intoxication" similar to those from alcohol, as well as depression and diminishing urinary output.)

🐾 Cocker Spaniel **DR. WATSON** loves winter, and not for the antifreeze! Winter is when he appears in his local Christmas pageant—as a Sheepdog.

Photo: G. & M. McCormack

53. Pronged collars can be good training tools.

Some people believe the pronged collar is a cruel way to keep me on a leash, and I agree—if you KEEP me in it, that is. The way I see it, some of us big guys don't know our own strength. We don't really know that we're pulling you around, especially when we get distracted. That pronged collar teaches us that we're tugging and helps us learn to heel. If used properly, it will only be necessary for "tune-ups" after a while. So take it from a big guy:

- Treat the pronged collar as a teaching tool, not a permanent walking collar. And make sure you choose the right size.
- Use it as a last resort, not a first step.
- Definitely, try the Gentle Leader headcollar first (Tip 8). It's designed to apply pressure not to our throats but to the back of our necks.
- And don't forget to try a standard harness.

🐾 Malamute/Red Husky–mix SKYE prefers an elegant leather leash—it looks great on her!

Photo: B. Bauman

Don't bother me,
I'm training.

54. We love puzzle toys—especially when there are treats involved.

Here's a fun present for a rainy day, especially for a dog like me who is big on chewing. Get one of my bones or a rubber Kong and fill it with peanut butter. I'll spend hours just trying to get it all out! (If I'm not into peanut butter, Kong actually makes fillings! Check them out at your pet store.) If you find that I really like this, you might want to invest in a toy that dispenses treats, like that puzzle ball to the left. They're great for when you have to leave me alone for extended periods of time!

🐾 **Irish Terrier AGNES has a backyard full of toys, chew balls, rawhide, and balls—and there's not a squirrel to be found!**

Photo: B. Corrigan, B. Sheehan

55. Learning basic commands is necessary before socializing.

There are so many things I will learn from socializing, but there are several commands I MUST know BEFORE you take me to a park.

"COME!" or whatever word you choose for "Get back here!"

"DOWN!" Sometimes I need to hear this command to help ward off aggressors.

"TREAT!" or "LOOK AT ME!" or my own name—whatever will get me to look at you and turn away from something—or someone—I shouldn't be focusing on.

I know they sound obvious, but my knowing these commands is for the good of every dog in the pack. If you can't get me to obey these commands easily, other dogs will see and hear your stress, and they might not respond in a good way.

🐾 ATTICUS is a beautiful Border Collie who lets his mom know how grateful he is that she rescued him with every sigh!

Photo: D. Chavez

56. Form a "neighborhood watch."

Find out which of your neighbors has experience with dogs and/or dog rescue, and learn how to rescue a stray. (Remember: you can't save ANY of us if you get hurt!) Get your other concerned neighbors to keep a "rescue pack" in their homes, complete with:

- A slip-on leash
- An easy-open can of dog food
- A pack of treats
- A bottle of water
- A water bowl
- The numbers of other neighbors who have experience and room for an overnight visitor

And be sure to put together a fund for your "lookout group," so that any dogs you rescue can be boarded while you look for a home.

🐾 She was rescued off the street by people who saw her and cared—and there is no better example of a dog worth saving than Black-and-Tan IVY, now home and loved!

Photo: A. Bobby

57. Even big dogs can fly!

Someday, you may need to fly me somewhere. If you and I need to fly and I am too big to stay in the cabin with you, then it's a good idea to check out both www.aspca.org and www.hsus.org to see the guidelines America's leading animal advocates suggest you follow.

That said . . . did you know that Continental Airlines is the first U.S. airline to be approved to fly dogs to the United Kingdom while eliminating the six-month quarantine? They also have a program called PetSafe that ships us not as checked baggage but as CARGO, with a dedicated 24-hour Live Animal Desk, constant monitoring of weather conditions, and online tracking!

And be on the lookout for Companion Air, the first airline created specifically for pets and their owners! When it takes to the skies, it will be the first airline with cabins designed just for me right next to yours. We'll even be able to visit with each other during flights! Watch for this new airline's launch at www.companionair.com.

 Bernese Mountain Dog HENRY and his owners were inseparable for ten years, so the thought of a six-month quarantine was scary for everyone. Flying Continental sure was better than hanging around in a kennel waiting to go home.

Photo: G. Hannon

58. Sticks and bones are always fun, especially when you get creative with them.

The next time you toss me a stick, think about tossing one of these:

- **A Brussels sprout stalk:** They're delicious, tough, and good for me.
- **Sugar cane:** What a special treat . . . I'll wonder what I've done to get such a present!
- **A carrot stick:** They're not just for rabbits anymore!
- **A bone:** Beef bones from the hip or knuckle of a cow will keep me gnawing for hours, and the marrow (especially in knuckle bones) is simply delicious—to me, anyway. Brisket bones are softer and I'll make them disappear completely! (Keep in mind, though, that too many bones can make me constipated. Make sure I poop the day after my treat—and NEVER give me cooked chop or chicken bones. They can splinter!)

🐾 Yorkie **THEODORE** is a huge carrot fan (baby carrots, please!), but he won't say no to broccoli, freeze-dried liver treats—or maybe a candy cane or two.

Photo: G. Staitti

59. If you spay me, I have a better chance of living a longer, healthier, and happier life.

Luckily, my owner loves me enough to have me spayed but, believe me, they don't call it "heat" for nothing. A girl who hasn't been spayed can go through hell. At least once a year, the intact female runs the risk of taking off in search of relief and, if she comes back, you can end up with a whole litter of pups in need of responsible care. She also runs a higher risk of breast cancer than does a spayed dog. Spaying your female means she won't get uterine cancer, ovarian cancer, or pyometritis, an infection of the uterus that can prove fatal. And don't believe the myth that says, "Going through one heat cycle is good for her health." Getting your female dog altered at about six months is a great way to keep her healthy. Then she can focus on the people she already loves—for a long time to come.

🐾 She was found running wild in a Baltimore park when she was two years old, but Doberman Pinscher JADE is gentle and dainty and much more suited to the loving home she's been living in ever since.

Photo: S. Caruso

60. Are your poop bags biodegradable?*

TWENTY-SEVEN MILLION TONS OF PLASTIC are thrown out—rather than recycled—in America every year. ONE MILLION TONS OF PLASTIC are recycled every year.

Some studies say that two million birds die every year from ingesting or getting tangled in plastic debris. They also say that one hundred thousand marine animals die the same way. Every year.

WE DOGS POOP. A LOT. EVERY YEAR.

There are now biodegradable waste bags available that COMPLETELY DECOMPOSE, when composted, in ten to forty-five days!

These bags can be composted in your backyard (if you have a compost system set up) or collected for your community composting center. Most communities collect biodegradable waste—ask your municipal center.

🐾 Other than on someone's lap, preferably in bed under the blankets, Miniature Dachshund SASHA's favorite place in the world is in a basket of clean laundry.

Photo: R. Silverman

Make sure the bags you buy meet ASTM D6400 standards. They should be made of corn-based renewable products, and no polyethylene should be used in the production process.

For more info, check out Biobagsusa.com and poopbags.com.

I KNOW how much you love me. Let's show Mother Earth how much we love her, too!

*By the way, you can avoid bags, biodegradable or otherwise, if you learn to just slide some newspaper under me right before I—well, you know. . . .

🐾 Fox Terrier MOLLY takes her walks VERY seriously—no scrap of food is safe from her!

Photo: W. Sims

TICKED OFF

61. Tick removal should be done safely—for everyone!

We spend a lot of time outside, so of course we sometimes get ticks. Lots of people try to remove ticks with blown-out matches, burning the tick with the hot match head, but this can REALLY BACK-FIRE, guys! People also panic if they don't get the entire tick out. The best way to remove a tick is with a tool specifically designed for the purpose (you can get it at your pet store) or with a pair of tweezers. If you don't get the whole tick out, don't worry. I may scratch at it a bit, but I'll be okay. Just use a little Betadine or antiseptic on the area to prevent a hot spot. And remember, ticks can carry diseases that are communicable to humans, so wash your hands thoroughly if you touch that tick!

🐾 No ticks on HORATIO! This Cocker Spaniel is the picture of health, and he should be—his mom is a veterinary assistant.

Photo: E Barrows

62. Here's a special training tip.

Okay, let's suppose I'm NOT perfect, and that there are some things I do that, well, you'd rather I didn't. And let's assume that you don't like yelling almost as much as I don't like being yelled at.

Lots of trainers will tell you that POSITIVE REINFORCEMENT is the key: giving me your support EVEN when I make a mistake—and giving me TONS OF SUPPORT when I DON'T make a mistake.

All you need is ready access to a treat (liver treats, boiled chicken bits, little bits of my favorite doggie snack) and REALLY GOOD TIMING!

Suppose I bark at other dogs on our walks, and you don't want me to. Maybe every time I bark you yank my leash and let me know you don't want me to do that.

But imagine if on our walks you give me praise—and the occasional treat—for all sorts of good things ("Good boy, you're not pulling!"

🐾 HARRY, a Shih Tzu, loves to be cuddled like a teddy bear, especially during thunderstorms!

Photo: L. Tenaglia

Havanese DAISY is such a smart girl, she remembers people, dogs, and any store where she's EVER gotten a treat.

Photo: C. Caroll

"Good girl, you're keeping me company, and I've had a really hard day!"). But then we run into another dog. And I bark. A LOT.

Try this. Don't yell. Just quietly give me some gentle words of support ("That was hard, but you're still a good dog!"), and keep walking with me, keep talking to me.

Eventually, I will be so full of treats and comfort that when a dog passes us, I won't bark.

THAT's when it's time to give me the most praise of all, and the most treats, AND a CODE: "GOOD dog—NO BARKING!"

Eventually, I'll realize that I never really let you down. I ALWAYS get praise and treats and love. But I get EVEN MORE praise and treats when I do the "NO BARKING" thing.

Positive reinforcement.

(This is just one simple lesson. A good dog-trainer knows LOTS of other things I can learn!)

HOTEL LE PAWS

63. Choose my kennel carefully and help make it feel like home.

Taking a trip? Am I staying in a hotel, too? It can feel like a vacation for me, too, you know, if you help make my kennel experience a pleasant one. Make sure the boarding facility you choose for me has a dog run and/or a team of good dog-walkers who will give me lots of quality time. Be sure to leave me with a few of my favorite toys (label them!), as well as things that smell like you (a blanket, a shirt, or a towel you've used), so I won't miss you so much. Check and see if the brand of kibble I like is the kind the kennel uses and, if it isn't, leave my brand; if I'm a "people-food" eater, arrange for a friend to come in and drop off my prepared meal. And while we're on the subject of those "friends" of yours, get a few people I know to drop in and visit me, especially if you are going to be gone awhile. (Be sure to make all appropriate arrangements with the kennel!)

🐾 **Standard Poodle BENNY will go anywhere—so long as his brother is nearby.**

Photo: R. Ulanet

64. Pure breeds need rescuing, too!

Thinking of getting a new Newfie? Know someone who wants a pure Peke? Don't go near that pet store! Did you know that the American Kennel Club has a Web site devoted to each recognized breed, where people post listings about dogs of all ages that have been displaced or are in need of adoption? You can help save the life of a dog in need of your love. Just visit the AKC Web site: http://www.akc.org.

Petfinder.com is also a great place to look. They work with thousands of adoption groups and can find you your dream dog based on everything from breed to location. Check them out!

🐾 Chihuahua PI was adopted from the San Francisco SPCA, and everyone who meets her agrees she is one of the more striking dogs they've ever seen!

Photo: D. Herman

65. The Exploding-Dog Diet

Okay, every once in awhile, we all get into something we shouldn't —in a big way! Whether it is a whole bowl of onion dip or a pan of brownies, we probably need some extra care after all of the cleaning up is done. Here's a great meal for the "post-party animal."

One part bland meat that's low in fat (such as chopped boiled chicken): this gives me simple protein.

Two parts white rice, boiled (some dogs prefer oatmeal): this gives me some bulk and fiber.

You can add some yogurt if I'm not lactose intolerant (see Tip 42).

A few days on a diet like this and I should be ready for my usual food (so long as it's not your pizza).

Don't forget, whenever I've had diarrhea for more than twenty-four hours, call my vet. And DON'T hesitate if you think I've eaten anything dangerous—see Tip 47 and get help!)

🐾 Yellow Lab/Pyrenee—mix **SNOOP** has eaten some strange things in his day, but with a face like his, he's **ALWAYS** forgiven!

Photo: L. McQuade

66. Have you checked my hearing?

So maybe I'm older than I look. We should all be so lucky.

And maybe I haven't been acting like myself lately, especially on walks. Have I been barking at strangers or tugging too hard on my leash? And maybe I've been downright grumpy or jumpy.

Well . . . MAYBE I don't hear you coming anymore. Maybe I'm worried that when we're walking, there's some dog behind us or across the street that I can't see or smell. Maybe I'm worried because I can't hear the traffic so well anymore and I don't want you to get hurt. Maybe I'm just missing the sound of your voice.

Ask the vet to check my hearing. It's a simple test and it might clear up a lot of stuff that's been going on. Unfortunately, there's not a whole lot we can do if I'm going deaf. But we can maybe take our walks at quieter times of the day, and you can wake me up differently. Maybe you could get me some Rescue Remedy, too (Tip 19). That will help me grow old more gracefully!

🐾 It's hard to know if Poodle DIJON is hard of hearing or just curious about dishwashers!

Photo: N. & A. Occhifinto

135

67. Ice is a great way to cool down our body temperature fast.

Here's a great treat for a hot summer day: Get a plastic container and fill it with water, then freeze it (leaving the top off). When I'm just lying around wishing it was snowing, give me my "frozen water bowl" to lick. This is also a great thing to take to the park, or for after play (once I've cooled down a bit). And it will keep those trips to the flushing water fountain down, too. (Boy, that toilet keeps the water nice and cold!)

🐾 **CHAUCER is a Soft-Coated Wheaten Terrier who loves being outside. That's where he herds all his friends!**

Photo: D. Gillman

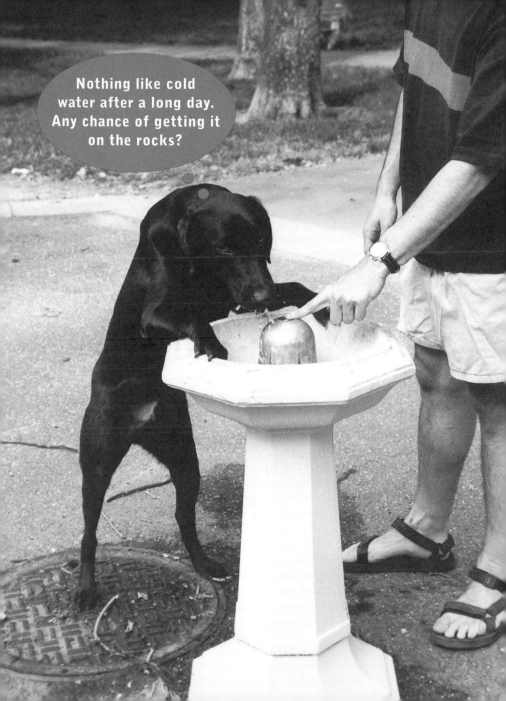

68. We depend on you to help us let go.

You've always said I tell you everything.

You've always said I talk to you and let you know what I'm thinking.

Well, there's one thing I'll never say. I will never tell you that I want to go. I will never tell you that it's time to say good-bye.

Not until you tell me it's okay.

And someday, I may need you to tell me that. I know you will, because there's no one in the world who loves me more. And there's no one in the world that loves you more.

I don't want you to hurt. I need to know that you're okay. I need to know that more than anything.

And then everything will be fine. I believe that. You should, too.

🐾 Tibetan Terrier **GEOFFREY** lived to be fifteen. He will always be both missed and loved.

Photo: Berg family

69. Onions are bad for me!

Okay, so you can't resist and you're going to give him a piece of that hamburger. It's meat, right? Good for him, right?

Let him have it—but HOLD THE ONIONS. Onions can damage red blood cells and cause hemolytic anemia. That's right. Onions. Cooked, uncooked, doesn't matter. Onions (and garlic, by the way) are a big no-no in a dog's diet, so next time you toss him a meatball, make sure that you know that what's in it won't hurt him.

🐾 When he's not playing tug-of-war with his family, Wheaten Terrier **FERGUS** is chewing the faces off all the toys in the house.

Photo: courtesy J. Thaler

70. Some of us new dogs just need a friend—and so do our owners.

You know the type: the dog who shows up at the dog run and reenacts the Battle of Gettysburg, or the puppy who turns up on the first day of obedience school and thinks it's one enormous bathroom.

You've seen him coming—that big, gallumphy dog bounding toward you on the street, a panicky owner trying desperately to keep up. Did you think to ask if everything was okay (even from the other side of the street)?

After a while, maybe you didn't see them anymore. Maybe they just gave up.

Lots of people adopt dogs that other people wouldn't, and they work VERY HARD to give them a happy life. These people—and these dogs—deserve compassion and support. AND YOUR EXPERTISE.

Look, you don't have to send your dog over to play. You don't even

🐾 Basset Hound LOUIS loves making new friends—
even ducks! He saved BARGAIN from being eaten by a
seagull and they've been best friends ever since!

Photo: L. Guy

🐾 **CHESTERFIELD**, an Akita/Shepherd mix, has come a long way from Times Square, where he was found. He now has a loving home and was trained at an early age to cheat at cards.

Photo: W. Dailey

have to come over yourself, if you're afraid. But you could contact an owner of a newer, more excitable dog. Talk to her without any dogs around. Share ideas. If you're comfortable enough, maybe bring your dog over for a "meet-and-greet"—maybe even with a trainer or behaviorist present. You can always share some of the tips in this book.

Some dogs, sadly, may not be able to function like other dogs. But lots of dogs' lives can be saved with patience and understanding— from all of us.

71. The primary ingredient in my food should be meat.

Did you know that I might be allergic to grain? My digestive system might have difficulty accepting the amount of grain you find in some brands of commercial dog food. If my diet contains kibble and canned food, make sure the main ingredient is MEAT. And I don't mean "meat by-products." (By-products are the parts of animals that are deemed unfit for human consumption, and "digest of by-product" is . . . well, you don't want to know.)

So bypass the by-product—and bring on the beef!

(And don't forget Tip 3—we might really like our meat RAW!)

 Husky BEAR loves his meat—almost as much as he loves taking a nap after eating!

Photo: C. Kies

72. Biting is necessary— controlling biting is the key!

Fact: Dogs bite things. Fact: Dogs NEED TO BITE THINGS. It's what we're meant to do. Fact: You can't stop me from biting—but you can stop me from biting what you don't want me to, and you CAN stop me from biting hard. The secret is giving me lots of toys to chew and bite—this lets me work out my biting instincts on things that have been approved by you. And let me know when my mouthing gets too tough. This will teach me to CONTROL the pressure of my biting, helping me develop a "soft mouth." Then we'll all be happy!

With her strong maternal instincts, nine-year-old mixed-breed BEE BEE is known as the "Hall Monitor" of her neighborhood park. She protects the little dogs and rescues them from rough play—when she's not chasing squirrels or swimming, that is.

Photo: Rick Reason, courtesy D. Seltzer

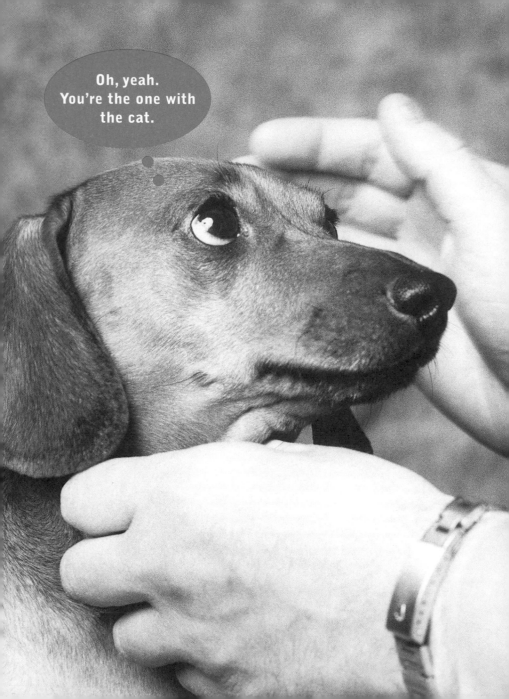

73. Smelling people is my way of shaking hands. Please let me go first!

Want to alleviate some of my anxiety? I know how good-looking I am, and I know all of your friends are nice. But I'd really like to get a good whiff of them before they go reaching to hug me and stuff. My nose tells me who they are a lot better than my eyes do. So, could you tell your friends and family to let me walk up to them and smell them first? If they hold out their hands to me, palm down, fingers in (like a closed paw), I'll be thrilled—and ready to play in no time at all.

Thanks. I knew I could count on you!

  Jack Russell BETTER knows what the mailman smells like. Here's how he found out!

Photo: L. Zazzi

74. The tiniest dogs have VERY special needs.

And I'm not talking sweaters (although they can be a BIG help)! There are an awful lot of dogs around these days that people like to call "teacups," although the AKC and reputable breeders do not recognize that word to describe an extremely small version of a breed. Chihuahuas under two pounds, Yorkies under two pounds, Poodles under three pounds, and—well, you get the idea—these are dogs whose adult weights are under the LOW end of their breed standard, and they require a great deal of care.

Did you know that the human equivalent to these teacups would be *less than thirty inches tall*? Imagine life at under three feet and you have a better understanding of how the world looks and feels and sounds to one of these dogs.

Maltese CB may look delicate and dainty, but give her some grass to roll around in (or, better yet, a pool to play in) and she's a wild thing!

Photo: Stark Naked Productions

🐾 Soft-Coated Wheaten Terrier WHISKEY is NO teacup at thirty-five pounds! He has an odd food ritual: removing ONE kibble bit from his bowl and laying it on the ground—preferably outside—before settling down to supper!

Photo: J. Libin

If you have a teacup, think twice before walking her where there are lots of cars and pedestrians and other dogs. Find a quiet street and a quiet time of day to walk your dog.

Teacups shouldn't be encouraged to jump too high—and for these dogs, that includes jumping onto furniture! Set up ramps and steps for your tiny dog; it will keep stress off of her fragile limbs and lower the risk of injuries.

Make sure she's not left alone for too long! If you work in a place where there's too much stress for such a little dog, make sure she's with someone who understands her needs and won't expose her to overwhelming situations.

Remember, she's small, but she's a dog and will put on a brave face for you. It's up to YOU to make sure your teacup is happy and healthy!

75. We are all unique, and wonderful to know.

So did you know we knew so much? Good for you. But let me remind you of another thing you probably know. No two dogs are alike. We are all magnificent, possessing individual gifts, with different likes, dislikes, fears, hopes, and ways of communicating. What's good for one of us may be unpleasant for another. You're the best judge of who your dog is and what your dog is saying to you. Enjoy your time together. See you in the park!

🐾 **COCOA** is a Chihuahua who loves to cuddle in Mom's large slippers. He loves to run and play fetch with his green ball, too.

Photo: Nancy DeJesus

Read More About Us

About Our Health

Fogle, Bruce, *First Aid For Dogs: What to do When Emergencies Happen,* New York: Penguin, 1997.

Griffin, James, *et al., Dog Owner's Home Veterinary Handbook,* Hoboken: Howell Book House, 2007.

Pitcairn, Richard H. and Pitcairn, Susan Hubble, *Doctor Pitcairn's Complete Guide to Natural Health for Dogs and Cats,* New York: Rodale Books, 2005.

Messonnier, Shawn, *Natural Health Bible for Dogs and Cats: Your A-Z Guide to over 200 Conditions, Herbs, Vitamins and Supplements,* New York: Three Rivers Press, 2001.

Messonnier, Shawn, *The Allergy Solution for Dogs: Natural and Conventional Therapies to Ease Discomfort and Enhance Your Dog's Quality of Life,* New York: Prima Lifestyles, 2000.

Zucker, Martin, *Veterinarians Guide to Natural Remedies for Dogs: Safe and Effective Alternative Treatments and Healing Techniques from the Nations Top Holistic Veterinarians,* New York: Three Rivers Press, 2000.

About Our Diet

Macdonald, Carina Beth, *Raw Dog Food: Make It Easy for You and Your Dog,* Wenatchee: Dogwise Publishing, 2003.

Moore, Arden, *Real Food for Dogs: 50 Vet-Approved Recipes to Please the Canine Gastronome,* North Adams: Storey Publishing, 2001.

Lonsdale, Tom, *Raw Meaty Bones Promote Health,* Wenatchee: Dogwise Publishing, 2001.

Palika, Liz *The Ultimate Dog Treat Cookbook: Homemade Goodies for Man's Best Friend* Hoboken: Howell Book House, 2005

About Our Behavior and Training

Donaldson, Jean, *The Culture Clash: A Revolutionary New Way to Understanding the Relationship Between Humans and Domestic Dogs,* Berkeley: James & Kenneth Publishers, 1997.

Rugaas, Turid, *On Talking Terms with Dogs: Calming Signals,* Wenatchee: Dogwise Publishing, 2005.

Monks of New Skeet, The, *How to Be Your Dog's Best Friend: The Classic Training Manual for Dog Owners,* New York: Little, Brown and Company, 2002.

Magazines and Newsletters About Us

The Whole Dog Journal
A monthly guide to natural dog care and training. GREAT for first-time dog owners, and a fascinating and informative read—you ALWAYS learn something new!

Dog Watch
A monthly newsletter from the Cornell School of Veterinary Medicine: the source for what VETERINARIANS want DOG OWNERS to know. Invaluable.

The Bark
A good resource for articles on behavior and health, with wonderful features and GREAT cartoons!!

Fido Friendly Magazine
A travel magazine for dogs and their owners, it explores dog-friendly travel destinations and much more.

Index

Acknowledgments

Thank you to all the dog owners and dog lovers who contributed to this book—your stories and photos were both inspirational and touching, and your dogs, a blessing. Cheers.

Special thanks to Clive Barker, the Newbern family, the Knight family, Elizabeth Barrows, Tom Berry, Shannon and David Kieske (and Lola), Catherine Bhone, Michael Cerveris, Griffin Dunne (and Gort), Sam and everyone at 4 and a Tail (especially Fluffy), Bobbie Giella, and the incomparable Polly Hanson.

I am deeply grateful to Rai Bernheim and Dr. Mark Gibson of Animal Kind Veterinary Hospital for helping me keep my facts straight, and to the entire staff for providing such excellent care to the pets of Park Slope—and their owners.

Thanks ad infinitum to Laura Ross for your scary-smarts, and for Moe and Mr. Finch.

Christopher Schelling . . . you had me at cow.

ANNE BOBBY is an actress with dozens of film, theater, and television credits to her name. She is a voice-over artist and narrator of audio books, as well as the coauthor of the play *That Woman: Rebecca West Remembers.* She is a longtime volunteer at the Brooklyn animal hospital where she takes her cats (yes, cats).

NEIL GAIMAN is the author of the New York Times-bestselling *American Gods, Anansi Boys, and Fragile Things*; the children's book *Coraline*; and the picture books *The Wolves in the Walls* and *The Day I Swapped My Dad for Two Goldfish.* He is also the author of critically acclaimed and award-winning short stories and novels for adults, including the legendary Sandman series of graphic novels. He wrote the scripts for the films *Mirrormask* and (with Roger Avary) *Beowulf.* Both *Stardust* (starring Robert De Niro, Michelle Pfeiffer, and Claire Danes) and *Coraline* (due out late 2008) have been adapted for the screen. Originally from England, Gaiman now lives in the United States with several cats, two beehives, and his rescued white German Shepherd, Cabal.